Warwickshire County Council
Warwickshire Publication

"First Published in February 2000 by Warwickshire Publications"

"Copyright to Warwickshire Publications"
Libraries and Heritage, Head Office, Barrack Street, Warwick CV34 4TH

Warwickshire Women

A Guide to Sources in the Warwickshire County Record Office

Rosalyn Foster and Christine Cluley

All rights reserved. No part of this publication may be reproduced, stored in a retrieval system, or transmitted in any form or by any means, electronic, mechanical, photocopying, recording or otherwise, without prior permission of the copyright holder.

ISBN No. 1 871942 19 5

Warwick Hiring Fair, 1872

Foreword

It is now over a quarter of a century since Sheila Rowbotham's *Hidden from History* was published and, if only British titles on women's history and gender studies are considered, it has been a period of great expansion. Perhaps it was educational history that first sparked popular interest in the subject, since career opportunities for females were so critically determined by their education, and this, except for the post-war grammar schools, had always been class-linked. However, women in history have traditionally been studied either through the famous heroines, exceptions to the rule - Elizabeth I, Florence Nightingale, the Brontës, Marie Stopes - or *en masse*, as mothers and workers, in this latter rule invariably in the humblest, most necessary and worst-paid occupations.

However, by skilfully exploiting archives, especially at a local level, women of all classes and backgrounds can be studied for themselves. Sometimes they fulfil a passive rôle in the sources - as patients, workhouse inmates, victims, employees, pupils, pauper apprentices - their lives arranged and their futures decided. Other females, even if only an unrepresentative minority, can be seen, even two centuries ago, directing their own and others' lives. Some women were clearly influential through their husbands, many were active partners in a family business, while labourers' wives invariably controlled the family budget. However, widows and spinsters were the only women in control of their own finances until the Married Women's Property Acts of the late nineteenth century. The emergence of women from the shadows of traditional history can be seen in this collection of sources held in the Warwickshire County Record Office. Some of these records will be found everywhere - quarter sessions, parish registers, census returns, newspapers. Others, however, although representative, are special to Warwickshire. Thus Dorothie Feilding's letters echo much to be found in Vera Brittain's correspondence, but are unique to her and her family. The treatment for insanity in 1734 was standard in medical practice for the period and would have been found in many overseers' collections. However, the very poor survival rate of such papers makes Catherine Clayton's bill a precious source, although she was only a passive participant.

This *Guide* suggests how sources can be traced, used and interpreted towards a better understanding of the changing position of women and their rules in society, especially in Warwickshire, across three centuries. It is to be welcomed not only as a research tool but as a view of individuals rather than of institutions in the past.

Joan Lane
Department of History
University of Warwick

Contents

Foreword	i
Contents	iii & iv
List of Illustrations	v & vi
List of Photographs	vi
Introduction	vii & viii
Acknowledgements	ix
Five Warwickshire Women	1
Lady Dorothie Feilding (1889 - 1935)	1
Minny Throckmorton (1832 - 1919)	8
Agnes Throckmorton (early seventeenth century)	10
Esther Tatnall (*c*. 1779 - 1857)	11
Eleanor Archer (1861 - 1960)	13
Broad Categories of Records	19
Letters	19
Poor Law Material	19
Local Newspapers	23
Census Returns	24
Institutional Records	25
Parish Records	27
Quarter Sessions Records	27
Directories	30
Records of Old-Established County Families	31
WCRO Library	33
Theses	34
Research Notes	34
Finding Women Through the Indexes	35
Subject Index	35
Accounts	35
Australia	35
Bastardy	38
Charities	38
Commonplace Books	38
Crime and Punishment	39

Contents (cont.)

Death	42
Diaries	42
Education	45
Food	46
Hospitals	48
Insanity	48
Labour	51
Libraries	51
Marriage	52
Medicine	52
Nonconformity	53
Nursing	54
Personal Papers	56
Registration, Civil	56
Textiles	56
War	60
Welfare	60
Women	60
Apprenticeship Index	66
Photographic Index	66
Wills Index	67
General Index	67
Personal Names Index	67
Property Index	68
Research by Alternative Strategies	71
Conclusion	75

List of Illustrations

All references are to sources at Warwickshire County Record Office

Frontispiece: Warwick Hiring Fair, 1872 (PV WAR Mar 5)	
Part of a letter from Lady Dorothie Feilding, 1915 (CR 2017/C581/68) Reproduced by kind permission of the Countess of Denbigh	5
Notice for Miss Eleanor Archer's Women's Employment Bureau (CR 367/46)	17
Part of a letter from Lady Penelope Mordaunt to her husband, Sir John, 9th January 1700 (CR 1368/1/22) Reproduced by kind permission of Sir Richard Hamilton	20
Settlement examination of Mary Prinsep, 1737 (CR 369/45/53)	21
A list of females in Warwick Workhouse, 1819 (DR 126/687)	22
Fashions for 5th April, 1806 in the *Warwick Advertiser*	24
Powder Certificates for Curdworth, 1795 (QS 16/1/4)	28
Victualler's Recognisance for Anne Harper, 1762 (QS 35/2/Box 10/697)	29
Calendar of Prisoners at Warwick House of Correction, 1801 (QS 26/2/2)	29
Mrs Satchwell's Tea-room, advertisement from White's *Directory*, 1874 (F. White & Co.'s *Directory* 1874, p.1432)	31
A page from Lady Anne Newdegate's accounts, 1600 (CR 136/B553) Reproduced by kind permission of Viscount Daventry	36
Emigration to New South Wales, 1833 (DR 583/98/2)	37

List of Illustrations (cont.)

Execution Poster of Mary Ball, 1849
(C 343 Lif (L) (p))   40

Pocket Book fashion plates, 1768 and 1801
(CR 136/A555 and A557)   41, 43

Page from Mary Wise's Recipe Book
(CR 341/301, p.41) Reproduced by kind permission of
P. Dennis Cole   47

Medicines for insanity, Shipston-on-Stour, 1734
(DR 446/82/1/1)   49

Letter to Jeffery Bevington Lowe, 1817
(CR 2926/37/1) Reproduced by kind permission of
Mrs M. Bayley   55

Eighteenth century household instructions
(CR 367/116/4)   62

Rules of the Society of Women, Kenilworth, 1798
(CR 2546/61) Reproduced by kind permission of
Local Studies Library, Coventry Libraries   64

Apprenticeship indenture, 1813
(DR 280/83/21)   65

List of Photographs

Cover photograph: Lady with a bicycle by Speight of
Nuneaton, c. 1900 (PH 352/215/50)

Lady Dorothie Feilding during the First World War
(CR 2017/F246/317, 326, 381) Reproduced by kind
permission of the Countess of Denbigh   3, 4

Clapham Terrace School, Leamington Spa, 1902
Reproduced by kind permission of Richard Neale   44

Warwick Laundry, 1930
(PH 352/187/284)   50

Women Workers during the First World War
(From *Women's Work* issued by the War Office,
September 1916 (CR 1520/box62))
  i)   Barrowing coke at a gas works   57
  ii)   Driving a goods delivery van   58
  iii) Brewery workers   59
  iv) Window cleaners   61

Suffragette March in Stratford-upon-Avon, 1913
(PH 350/2227, 2228)   63

Introduction

The main aim of the Warwickshire County Record Office (WCRO) is to make its resources available for study. This is incorporated in the County Council's wider vision of encouraging the general public to use and enjoy what is their heritage. *Warwickshire Women* has been written for those who are interested in the history of women and to make them aware of the valuable deposits in the archives of the WCRO.

There is a wealth of material about women in their family roles, in trade, industry and the professions, waiting to be discovered, and, because women's history has been largely ignored until recently, the field is wide open. This publication should appeal to the general reader, but it is hoped that it will inspire a deeper interest and promote the desire to investigate further. With the emergence of women's history as a contemporary discipline at an advanced level of study, it will help students to exploit primary sources.

Although using original documents is exciting and often rewarding, it is not always an easy task and obtaining access to the material is not necessarily straightforward. In the WCRO there is no single collection labelled 'Women' because the archive material cannot be organised thematically. There are, however, between four and five thousand separate collections, nearly all of which were created as by-products of some activity in the past, and that are now being used for historical research; they rarely in themselves answer all researchers' questions. There will be material about women in many of these collections, and researchers need to think laterally to discover information. This *Guide* is intended to make the task easier.

The first five studies are each an example of the large amount of information that can be revealed by use of the archives. Next come descriptions of the broad categories of documents. We believe that such explanations are helpful to new users, and remove the awe that is often inspired by specialist information. The *Guide* continues with a selection from the very large Subject Index followed by brief entries from other indexes. The final section offers advice on various different ways to find information on elusive subjects both inside the WCRO and beyond.

Warwickshire Women is comprehensive but not definitive, and readers should remember that the selected references are meant to be representative of the collection as a whole. However, we hope that all readers will enjoy the contents, and will be encouraged to visit the County Record Office to make their own discoveries.

Acknowledgements

We have thoroughly enjoyed researching and writing this *Guide* but without the help of others it would not have evolved from its initial stages. We would like to thank the following for their ideas, support and great enthusiasm: Louise Hampson and Monica Ory, past archivists at the WCRO; all the present staff; Dr. Joan Lane and Professor Carolyn Steedman of Warwick University. Thanks are also due to Mary Smith for proof reading and to Mo Thomas for editorial assistance. In particular, we are grateful to Chris Jeens, former County Archivist, for his skilful direction of this project.

Five Warwickshire Women

Lady Dorothie Feilding
(1889-1935)

Lady Dorothie was the second daughter of the Earl of Denbigh of Newnham Paddox, and served with the Munro Ambulance Corps in Flanders from 1914 until her marriage to Captain Charles Moore of Mooresfort, Tipperary, in July 1917.

About two hundred and fifty of Dorothie's letters home during this period are contained within the Feilding collection,[1] and they present a detailed and vivid picture of life at the front. The correspondence was, with the exception of a few letters to her father, mostly addressed to her mother, and was often a hurried scrawl in an intimate and conversational style, which lent the letters a startling freshness and immediacy.

Many aspects of her daily life were included in her writing; she gave eye-witness accounts of air-raids and shelling and descriptions of the perilous work of collecting casualties and driving them to hospital, often under fire. She told stories about her pet terrier, Charles, made rude remarks about the military censors, and commented on the beauty of the wild poppies and cornflowers she saw growing near the battlefields.

She had a deep sense of patriotism and was determined to 'do something' in the war; she seemed to have experienced real exhilaration at being so close to the fighting and, like many young women of her class, revelled in her new-found freedom. Her resilience and cheerfulness, her use of current expressions such as 'ripping' and 'topping', and her utter contempt for cowardly conduct, make her both appealing and formidable.

After a short training course at Rugby Hospital in August 1914, Dorothie was at Ghent by the end of September with Dr Munro's British Red Cross Motor Ambulance Corps, helping to feed thousands of hungry soldiers,[2] and encountering difficulties in obtaining petrol for their large motor ambulances (one was a 40hp Daimler with solid tyres).[3]

After the fall of Antwerp, Ghent had to be evacuated and Dorothie wrote angrily from Dunkirk, where all was chaos; '...I have had to run the whole dam [sic] show...'.[4] She describes Munro as 'losing his silly head and running round in circles',[5] and they feared they would be sent back to England. Dorothie's chance encounter with an acquaintance who was a relative of Baron de Broqueville, the Belgian War Minister, changed the fortunes of the Munro Ambulance Corps, as he used his considerable influence to help Dorothie and her colleagues. A field hospital was to be set up at Furnes, and Munro's Corps was to feed it. Dorothie was delighted at the outcome: 'Ripping and I'm so glad we have a job'.[6]

Dorothie undoubtedly cut a dashing figure and became something of a celebrity quite early in her war career, much to her annoyance. She was furious that reporters were allowed to go out with the ambulances and felt that *The Chronicle* unfairly played up her rôle in its account of the evacuation of Dixmude in October 1914, where they evaded the advancing Germans by ten minutes.[7]

The following year Dorothie was working as hard as ever, but felt that her position in the Ambulance Corps was insecure. She was relieved when the English Mission wrote to her in April and granted her official permission to stay and 'will not oppose it in any way and have written to the Red Cross to say so'.[8]

Lady Dorothie Feilding during the First World War.

Lady Dorothie Feilding during the First World War.

Furnes
26.9

Mother dear · It's so odd to be back in the same old place doing the same old things - same old odors, same old faces, same old late nights, same old everything. It's very nice though to be doing something & entirely a _degree_ of hate. I hated going away from home & coming back, but I should hate far more to have nothing to do at home, so have no grievance at all really. Each time one gets the joy of a real good lay at home & is tempted perhaps to chuck things up, one realises it's only because it's temporary that "breath mats" are so very pleasant. & of all the jobs going in war time I think I have the best. Perhaps hard in some ways, but it is most

Part of a letter from Lady Dorothie Feilding from the Front in Flanders, June 1915.

She received two decorations in 1915; in February she was made a Knight of the Order of Leopold of Belgium, and in May she was mentioned in despatches, for which she was awarded the Croix de Guerre. Although she relished the danger of her work and would have found routine nursing dull, the strain and discomfort began to take their toll, and in May she wrote to say that she had spent a day by the sea,[9] that she had been for a ride on the sands on a borrowed 'gee',[10] and stayed with the de Broquevilles at the Chateau de Weez.[11]

Later in the year her health appeared to have broken down and she returned home for an extended leave of two months. She had been greatly affected by the scenes she had witnessed. 'It just despairs one and makes one rage when you see this endless endless stream of shattered humanity, and see the ghastly work a shell can make of their poor bodies...'[12] Although she was a devout Roman Catholic, these experiences destroyed her faith in an afterlife: 'I think that there is just an endless blank that begins after death and that all things finish there. I try to believe that there is a future, but I can't any more'.[13]

In January 1916 she made arrangements for her mother and 'Squeaker', her younger sister, Clare, to come over and visit her at the front. She has advice on packing for 'Squeaks': 'No evening kit or tea gown needed... Just coats and skirts and a good warm motor coat...'[14] She is immensely excited at the prospect of seeing her family again. 'What fun we will have - I will smuggle you up here for a few days and knock off work, as you won't be allowed in the lines now, it's much stricter... In fact if you or Squeaker feel it isn't warlike or exciting enough and disappoints you, I will sprinkle a few barbed wire entanglements round the bedroom, remove the mattress and the soap - break a window or two etc - In fact anything to please you...'[15]

After the visit there was more excitement: Dorothie and her colleagues have been given a black swan to eat. 'Cooking swan has a most curiously penetrating smell - everything one touches from British warms to pyjamas has a pungent swan odour attached...'[16]

Early in 1917 Dorothie was complaining about the mud, the cold and the gas attacks. 'It's a dirty business gas and rather frightening - comes in great foggy waves and makes you cough your head off.'[17] The marriage to Charles seemed to have been arranged quite rapidly, and Dorothie began to look forward to leaving the war behind. 'I need just a little bit of peace and happiness so badly...'[18]

In June she returned to Flanders on active service for the last time; she had deliberately chosen dangerous work and had proved herself gallant and courageous. In one of her last letters to the Countess she wrote about the past three years: 'Here right at the heart and pulse of things one finds realities and greatness'.[19]

Minny Throckmorton
(1832-1919)

This is an unusual and interesting collection of letters, telegrams, photographs and memorabilia sent to Mary Throckmorton, known as Minny, from various members of the Habsburg court in the late nineteenth century. There are portraits of members of the Austrian royal family, letters on the suicide of Crown Prince Rudolph in 1889 and the assassination of Empress Elizabeth in 1898, as well as many charming letters from the Archduchess Marie-Valerie when a child.

In 1868 Mary Throckmorton, eldest daughter of Sir Robert Throckmorton of Coughton, 8th Baronet, received a letter from Elizabeth, wife of Franz Joseph, Emperor of Austria, inviting her to become lady-in-waiting and governess to her youngest child, the Archduchess Marie-Valerie, who had been born that April.[20] Mary appears to have travelled widely on the Continent, and the Throckmortons had many European connections through family and friends.

The letter from the Empress in 1868 to Miss 'Frockmorton' invited Minny to take charge of the education of her 'beloved little Valerie', and was the beginning of a stream of letters from the Habsburg Court which ended only with Minny's death in 1919. After she had left the court Marie-Valerie sent Minny about 110 letters beginning in 1876 with Christmas and New Year greetings, and thanks for presents on her birthday and nameday, sometimes with a small drawing or painting enclosed. There is one of her cat, about whom she writes later that he became so wild that he had to be sent to the palace menagerie.[21] Later on Minny was sent a beautiful Christmas card with a picture of a basket of violets.[22]

Also in the collection are telegrams, invitations, menus, the Archduchess's wardrobe inventory, Minny's Star Cross Order and the Order of St. Elizabeth, together with a passport of 1871. Some of the correspondence has interesting monograms and seals.

There are several letters to Minny after the suicide of Crown Prince Rudolph and the murder of Marie Vetsera at Mayerling in January 1889. Marie-Valerie wrote to her in May, referring to the tragic events as a 'misfortune', and saying that her mother's health had been affected.[23] A friend, G.E. Buchanan, wrote relaying court gossip in the wake of the scandal. Referring to Marie Vetsera's parents, the writer says, '...one felt he was not of the best, and I did not like her at all, such bad style. The Baltazzi father who had made the money which brought them all forward was, I heard, a wool merchant'. In September 1898 another tragedy befell the Austrian royal family when the Empress Elizabeth was assassinated in Switzerland. Marie-Valerie writes to Minny in November of 'the dreadful blow'. There is also a breathless letter in French from Marie Festetics, lady-in-waiting to the late Empress.[24]

Agnes Throckmorton
(Early Seventeenth Century)

Agnes Throckmorton appears as a sharp-tongued and forthright correspondent in a short series of letters written between *c.* 1607 and 1612. Agnes, née Wilford, widow of John Throckmorton, wrote concerning the affairs of her son, Robert, who became the first baronet in 1642. Agnes was prepared to take a firm line when it came to family matters, as can be seen in the first letter, which was to her father-in-law, Thomas (1533-1615). In it she was furious with him for attempting to arrange a marriage for Robert without her knowledge. 'You may conceve your self whether it wolde not greve a mother that hath broght a childe into the worlde with grefe, paine, and danger of my life, to have any caus geven to think that I shoulde be made a stranger in his bestowing...' [25]

In a second letter to Thomas, written in January 1607/8, there was a plan to send Robert 'beyonde the seas', and her previous intervention must have had its desired effect as Agnes remarked that 'this late marriage is broken'.[26] The fifth letter of the series was written to Robert and his wife and was undated. The young couple had been ill, and Agnes hoped that they would soon be able to leave London because 'that smoky are did never agree with nether of you...' She ended by voicing her worries over the safety of Thomas Throckmorton, who, as a member of a leading Catholic family after the Reformation, was liable to persecution.[27]

In a final angry letter that Robert in his reply called 'sharpe', she berated him at length for keeping racehorses. Like many parents she was worried about what the neighbours would say: '... this mater hath been longe in hand but very carfully kept from me till all the contrye talketh of it that Papist hath so much monis that they run it away...' She complained bitterly that he never listened to her 'I have long founde my self and my best advise so littel regarded by you...' Her great concern was, of course, that Robert's estate will be frittered away on 'runninge horsis', but she thought that nothing she said would make any difference: 'I verily thinke it will worke no impression in you.'[28]

Esther Tatnall
(*c*.1779-1857)

Arriving at Warwick Gaol with her husband, the new Governor, on her wedding day in 1803, Esther Tatnall was appalled by what she saw of the miserable and overcrowded conditions that then prevailed. In the account she wrote of her experiences at the gaol, which was published in *Topographical Tracts* in 1836, she recalled hearing the clanking of chains as she entered 'this abode of wretchedness'. After having temporarily escaped to her father's house in Kineton she was recalled to her duty of supporting her husband in his work, and embarked upon an arduous twenty-three-year-long career of dedicated prison reform.

This was a formidable task for a twenty-four-year-old woman, but she displayed courage, compassion and great fortitude in the face of indifference from the prisoners and what she called 'cold disregard' from the authorities.

With about twenty women inmates she initiated Bible-reading and prayer sessions, eventually winning their confidence and helping them to employ their time usefully in washing and mending. After some ten years she was allowed to work with the girls aged from about ten to twelve, and organised the teaching of reading and the catechism. The boys younger than sixteen were also taken under her wing, and again she had them taught to read, although they suffered from a lack of books.

In 1814 the incoming magistrates recognised her work and allotted funds for the proper equipping of a school-room, while hot and cold baths and adequate clothing were now provided for prisoners. Esther investigated possible employment for the boys and chose the heading of pins as suitable, which gave them a little income. Adults were employed first on lace-running and then on the sticking of patten ties.

In 1815 her efforts were duly rewarded by the magistrates, and she was presented with a plated teapot bearing an inscription mentioning her 'meritorious conduct' towards the prisoners. People of importance began to hear about Esther's work, and among eminent visitors to the gaol were Elizabeth Fry, in 1823, as well as two royal princesses and many notables who were passing the season at nearby Leamington.

The strain of so many years of demanding work affected the health of both Esther and her husband, and she was greatly relieved when, in 1823, a matron was appointed for the females and in the following year a new chaplain installed who superintended the schools. In 1826 Tatnall retired, and survived only four more years. Esther was left badly off and forced to apply to the magistrates for financial help, which they were unable to grant.

From 'A Narrative of 23 Years' Superintendence of the Women and Boys' Wards in the Gaol at Warwick' by Esther Tatnall, Widow of the late Governor, in *Topographical Tracts*, edited and with an introduction by Sir E. Eardley Wilmot in 1836. (A. TOP)

Eleanor Archer
(1861-1960)

Eleanor Archer was the daughter of Joseph and Susannah Tedney Archer. Her father was a farm labourer, later a farm manager. She was baptised at Warton, Warwickshire, and in January 1864 the family moved to Hunningham, where her father became farm bailiff. In 1886 they were living at Moreton Hill Farm, Moreton Morrell, and in October 1886 had moved to The Poplars, Sherbourne. Her mother was buried at Sherbourne on 12 May 1888, aged sixty-three; her father remarried and had several more children. Miss Archer was educated at Hunningham National School and by her mother, a former headmistress. She did not need to work for her living, but was able to choose her occupations. These and her interests, which were many, reflect the optimistic Victorian moral outlook that prevailed at the time. She belonged to the Temperance Movement and had a keen interest in the improvement of mankind in general, a strong social conscience, and was a believer in self-help. She was also deeply religious and was a member of the Band of Hope. Her political convictions were reflected by her membership of the Primrose League which was an organisation formed to spread Conservative principles. Her wide variety of interests is reflected in the many magazines in the collection. A few examples are listed below:

The Herald of Salvation
Bible Stories for Young Readers
The Church Worker
Band of Hope Review
The Church of England Chronicle
The Parlour Magazine of the Literature of all Nations.
Mother and Home
The Vegetarian
Bond of Brotherhood

She was an Assistant Overseer and Collector of Poor Rates from Barford from 1892 until 1924 or 1928. The family was friendly with Joseph Arch; she rented his cottage in Barford and was there in 1895. Joseph Arch founded the National Agricultural Worker's Union in which, as Frances, Countess of Warwick, writes, 'the legitimate discontent of the agricultural labourer found its legitimate outlet'. Arch's efforts to achieve recognition and rights would have appealed to Miss Archer's sense of justice. The conditions of the farm labourers were exacerbated by the devastating agricultural depression that began in the 1870s and continued for over thirty years. Many labourers and their families were driven into the towns to seek work. Domestic service was the biggest employer of women, and Miss Archer involved herself with this by running a servants' registry from her home in Victoria Street, Warwick, *c.* 1910 - 20. The contribution of farmers' wives and daughters is rarely mentioned in nineteenth-century agricultural accounts but they played an important part in dairying because well-prepared butter and cheese attracted high prices. Also, the care of poultry and sale of eggs were usually the responsibility of the women. In the 1880s there was a growing concern about the variable quality of much of the dairy produce from British farms, and the poor standards of hygiene associated with its manufacture. In 1880 the Bath and West of England Society held a ten-day dairying course at Swindon, and other similar courses followed. All early courses concentrated on butter making; a cheese school was not established until 1890.

One of Miss Archer's many interests was literature. She was very widely read and corresponded with friends, encouraging their literary criticism. She started a circulating booklet entitled '*The Quiver Manuscript Magazine*', inviting contributions of poems, articles on natural history, gospel tracts, works about temperance and newspaper articles. Politics were excluded. She also wrote reports and articles for the local press. Another interest was local politics, and she was a firm supporter of the Labour Party. She applied for the appointment of Inspector under the Shop Hours Act in 1898, but, although very highly recommended and with excellent testimonials, she was unsuccessful. One of her most fascinating interests and involvements was with the Viavi Cause.

This was concerned with health problems particular to girls reaching puberty and women. The Viavi Cause was founded in San Francisco by two brothers, Herbert L. and Hartland Law, who claimed it was 'the greatest power for making women sound'.

The Viavi Gynaecological Plates were designed to educate mothers and daughters on the diseases of the uterine organs. The business was conducted on a solely educational basis, and the product was not sold through commercial channels. It was a home remedy, and established in every community by a home resident who was one of a great army of educators, one of whom, in England, was Eleanor Archer. The treatment and philosophy followed modern homeopathic principles, and was not just medicinal. The philosophy was holistic and took into account the whole person, her mental attitudes and values. There was a responsibility to 'spread the good word', and shape the progress of the race and the destiny of the world.

Every known medicinal herb, drug, fruit and flower from many places in the world was sent to the laboratory and went through various processes such as percolating, treating, and mixing. Women workers created a vegetable compound whose final shape was 'Tablettes' packed in glass tubes with antiseptic absorbent cotton, and wrapped in paper to exclude light. 'Every well-informed woman is aware that eighty per cent of the women confined in asylums for the insane owe their unhappy lot to uterine troubles... No woman who is not perfectly balanced is capable of producing a perfect child'. These views reflect the Victorian moral climate and optimism, which taught that if people were clean-living, virtuous, God-fearing, and temperate mankind's lot would improve.[30]

Education for women was also highly valued. More importantly, these views suggest it is the responsibility of women to bring about the improvements. If they were healthy they should be able to perform the tasks for which they were suited. Miss Archer obviously wholeheartedly supported this philosophy. She lived in Warwick from *c.*1909 until her death in 1960.[29]

REFERENCES

Lady Dorothie Feilding
General

CR 2017/C580/1 - 61, CR 2017/C581/1 - 159, CR 2017/C582/1 - 109, CR 2017/C583/1 - 85. See also letters sent home by Lady Dorothie's sister, Lady Marjorie Feilding, who nursed the wounded at the Edinburgh and Border Hospital, Dunkirk, from the beginning of the war until her marriage to Captain Edward Dudley Hanly in February 1915, CR 2017/C588/1-37. Feilding Family Photograph Albums, 1888, CR 2017/Y5,6. See also CR 2017/F236 - 256, pp. 126 - 128 of list for her personal papers.

[1] CR 2017
[2] CR 2017/C580/8
[3] CR 2017/C580/9
[4] CR 2017/C580/12
[5] CR 2017/C580/15
[6] CR 2017/C580/13
[7] CR 2017/C580/21
[8] CR 2017/C581/31
[9] CR 2017/C581/46
[10] CR 2017/C581/54
[11] CR 2017/C581/52
[12] CR 2017/C581/42
[13] CR 2017/C581/152
[14] CR 2017/C582/2
[15] CR 2017/C582/3
[16] CR 2017/C582/13
[17] CR 2017/C583/36
[18] CR 2017/C583/55
[19] CR 2017/C583/55

Miss Eleanor E Archer's
High Class Registry Office
and
Information Bureau.

HOURS:

Ladies: Mondays, 2 to 4.
Servants: Each Evening, 7 to 8.
Saturdays, 4 to 6.

Notice for Miss Eleanor Archer's Women's Employment Bureau

Minny Throckmorton

General

CR1998/Tribune/Folder 24: letters and journal of Miss Mary (Minny) Throckmorton

CR1998/Tribune/Folder 27: letters mainly to Miss Mary Throckmorton

CR1998/Larger Veneered Box: Miss Mary Throckmorton: miscellaneous correspondence

CR1998/Small Showcase in the Saloon: letters from Habsburg court to Miss Mary Throckmorton

[20] CR 1998/Small Showcase in Saloon/14/1-14
[21] CR 1998/Larger veneered box 'The Empress'/1876 - 1891
[22] Misc. Bundle
[23] CR 1998/Small Showcase in Saloon/11
[24] CR 1998/Larger Veneered Box

Agnes Throckmorton

General

CR 1998/Box 60/1 - 6

[25] CR 1998/Box 60/Folder 1/1
[26] CR 1998/Box 60/Folder 1/2
[27] CR 1998/Box 60/Folder 1/5
[28] CR 1998/Box 60/Folder 1/6

Eleanor Archer

General

CR 367

[29] CR 367/13/1 Diary, 'A Month in the Country' was written at Harbury Fields Farm. CR 367/15/1. From: *Technical Education in Dairy Work* - Dairy Farm School, Halloughton Hall, Whitacre. Aim of school - to provide thoroughly efficient teaching in the theory and practice of butter and cheese-making.

Broad Categories of Records

LETTERS

These range from individual items to several large series of letters, from business to highly personal correspondence, and can be valuable sources of information.

A good starting-place for locating letters is in the records of old-established county families mentioned below, which are listed in the WCRO catalogues.[1]

From a huge amount of personal correspondence, Lady Dorothie Feilding's letters to her mother and father are outstanding, and offer a lively commentary on her experiences at the front during the First World War.[2]

Agnes Throckmorton's acerbic letters to her son in the early seventeenth century illustrate her concern about his way of life. It is interesting to note that little has changed regarding parents' perceptions of their responsibilities.[3]

POOR LAW MATERIAL

The Elizabethan Poor Law was passed in 1601 as an attempt by the state to deal with pauperism. The poor were divided into four groups: the old, sick and infirm; the deserving poor; children; vagrants and the idle poor. Legislation required that each parish

A letter from Lady Penelope Mordaunt to her husband, Sir John,
9 January 1700

was responsible for its own poor and should elect Overseers to levy a parish rate with which to provide outdoor relief for the able-bodied and bed, board and care to the rest. The Overseers had to provide tools, material and work for the able-bodied.

In 1662 the Stuart Parliament passed the Settlement Laws, which sought to prevent strangers, particularly pregnant women and able-bodied men, from settling in parishes other than their own.

Settlement Examination of Mary Prinsep, 1737

In 1782 Gilbert's Act, which was not compulsory but could be adopted, empowered groups of adjacent parishes to build Union workhouses for their sick and infirm; these were run by paid guardians. Outdoor relief for the deserving poor was continued.

The system came under more and more pressure, attempting to deal with the increasing costs of poverty. Wholesale reform came with the Poor Law Amendment Act of 1834, which established a national system of Poor Law Unions. The gradual introduction of state responsibility led to the repeal of the Poor Law Act in 1927.

Workhouse belonging to the Parish of Warwick. Taken November 19th 1819.

Nº	Females	Age	Infirmities	Came into House	How Employd	Left the House	When died
1.	Mary Harris	51		April 24th 1810	Clean the their Rooms	Dec. 20. 1819	
2.	Ann Barnett	55	Cripple	Sept. 30th 1814	Washing Makes the Beds	Sept 5 1823	
3.	Elizth Moore	50	Rheumatism	July 14th 1811	do	Feby 15th 1820	
4.	Sarah Baker	21		April 24th 1810	Go's out Nursing	May 14	
5.	Phoeby Wills	27		July 1st 1819	Nurse the Child	May 4	
6.	Sarah George	40	Lunatic	Sept. 5 1812			
7.	Elizth Job	25		June 6th 1817	Nurses her Child	May 4 1821	
8.	Cathe Sabin	20		Nov. 18 1816	Spins	June 15	
9.	Mary Hale	20	Cripple	July 29th 1819	Knits	June 3	
10.	Ann Allen	60	Ideot	1774			
11.	Elizth Toney	60	do	1779			
12.	Sarah Bromage	70	Childish	1784			June 9 1820
13.	Mrs Walton	60	Lunatic	Feby 9th 1819		Oct. 22 Sent to Bethnal Grn	
14.	Sarah Hitchcox	58	do	1801			
15.	Ann Lowke	53		Nov. 21 1812	Jn. Cutting Rooms		
16.	Ann Upton	23	Ill	April 17 1819			Dec. 29 1819
17.	Harrt Culverwell	20		Nov. 5 1819	Put to Bed	Jany 9th 1820	
18.	Ann Crook	60	Ideot	1779			
19.	Sarah Hinton	64		Oct. 5 1810	Go's out Nursing	died Aug. 1820	
20.	Sarah Moore	20	Cripple	Aug 14th 1811	Schoolmistress	Feb 15th 1820	
21.	Charlt Morris	17		July 27 1811	Spins	Aug. 12 1821	
22.	Harrt Hopkins	16		Sept 20. 1812	Go's out Nursing	May 4	
23.	Elizth Hancox	15		1804	Spins	May 11 1822	
24.	Phoebe Hale	14		July 29 1819	In Cutting Room	May 8	
25.	Martha Barnett	13		April 30 1810	Go's out Nursing	July 31 1823	
26.	Margaret Mare	12		April 23	Knits	June 20 1822	
27.	Eliza Hopkins	9		May 5 1819	do	June 5 1823	
28.	Ann Hopkins	14		April 29 1819	Spins		
29.	Sarah Smith	13		April 20 1817	do	Feb. 4 1822	

Carrd Forwards

A list of females in Warwick Workhouse, 1819.

The following Poor Law material held at the WCRO is useful for the study of women's history: (pre 1834) Settlement Examination Certificates, Removal Orders, Overseers' Accounts, Bastardy Bonds and Affiliation Orders. For later information (post 1834) see the Guardians of the Poor Minute Books, the Admission and Discharge Registers and the General Ledgers. [4]

The Overseers' account books give much detailed evidence of the lives of the inmates of local workhouses. In a volume marked 'Ledger Commencing 1816 - 1818, No 1' for Warwick St Mary, there are lists of receipts and disbursements for rents, meat, flour and other necessary items. There is also a 'List of Poor' in the workhouse on 18 November 1819, giving their names, ages, infirmities, dates of entry and employment. These records also show that women were employed in the workhouses as midwives, nurses and seamstresses.[5]

Women are often mentioned in the Settlement Examinations, where there are examples of their being dismissed without references, unmarried pregnancies and other difficult circumstances.

LOCAL NEWSPAPERS

The WCRO holds several sets of newspapers, some of which are on microfilm. There are complete sets of the *Warwick Advertiser* and the *Nuneaton Chronicle*.[6]

In 1806 the *Warwick Advertiser* was running a monthly column on current ladies' fashions. In February, the Circassian turban was the *haut ton*. The Trafalgar dress hat is mentioned as a possible long-term fashion. However, 'beads mixed with the hair are considered quite *mauvais ton*'.

Whenever an important event had taken place at Court, the newspaper recorded in minute detail all the costumes of those present. At the celebration for Queen Charlotte's birthday in January 1806, Her Majesty wore puce-coloured velvet with gold acorn tassels. The acorn motif was in vogue and Princess Agusta's (*sic*) white crepe gown was adorned, not only with acorn tassels, but also with oak and acorn bunches.

The reading of these reports gives some idea of the sumptuous apparel worn by the very wealthy, and was one of the ways in which ordinary women could learn about the highest and latest fashions.

The newspapers include job vacancies for women, advertisements for establishments run by women (such as schools) and advertisements aimed at women, especially milliners and dressmakers. The *Rugby Advertiser*, 10 November 1860 contains an advertisement for 'Female Christie Minstrels offering refined Negro Music'.

CENSUS RETURNS

A national census was first carried out in 1801, and has been conducted at ten-yearly intervals ever since. The exception was 1941, when a census was not taken because of the war.

FEMALE FASHIONS FOR APRIL

FULL DRESSES.—A loose robe of undressed crape over a dress of white satin or sarsenet, embroidered all round with silver; the sleeves quite plain, and embroidered to correspond with the dress. A tiara of silver, or steel, adorned with gems or cornelians. White gloves and shoes.—A round dress of fine muslin over white sarsenet. Broad lace let in down the front and round the bottom. The bosom quite plain, trimmed with a quilling of lace, and ornamented with a medallion or broach. A long silk shawl, the ends embroidered in colours. The hair dressed with a bandeau of velvet and diamonds.

HEAD DRESSES.—A turban made of an Indian shawl, ornamented in front with a medallion —A turban of very thin muslin, finished with a long end from the top—A small round cap of thin muslin, the front ornamented with worked vine leaves—The hair dressed with a tiara—A morning dress of thick white muslin, made up close to the throat with a collar. Necklace and armlets of cornelian. A straw hat turned up in front.

GENERAL OBSERVATIONS.—The favourite colours are pea-green, lilac and yellow. Spring pelisses, of soft silk of various colours, are worn, but not generally. Spencers and mantles are more worn. Feathers have almost entirely disappeared, both in full and undress. Small wreaths of flowers painted on lace, are much used for the dress of the head.

Fashions for April, 1806, in the Warwick Advertiser

Before 1801 there might have been an occasional census, usually in a parish collection, but there was no consistent policy on execution. Returns are sometimes entered in parish registers, when either households with heads only are listed, or just population totals. Between 1801 and 1841 incumbents sometimes took censuses listing the household or simply giving population totals.

The first four national censuses from 1801 to 1831 survive only in statistical form, with a few exceptions. More detailed returns date from 1841, when further information was required, but only stating whether or not a person was born in the county. As the century progressed, more details were added; for example, the census of 1851 included the place of birth and the current address was required, but not always recorded. Other information included the names of members of the household and their relationship to the head, their ages, sex, whether married or unmarried, occupation, place of birth, and whether they had any disability such as deafness, dumbness, blindness or insanity. They are therefore very useful resources for discovering much about women's history.

The WCRO holds the census returns for most places in Warwickshire for 1841 to 1891 and also from some parishes that are in neighbouring counties. These are now held either on microfilm or on microfiche, depending on the date.[7]

INSTITUTIONAL RECORDS

These cover numbers of different types of institutions including hospitals, lunatic asylums, schools, prisons and workhouses. The information cannot be found in one single collection; it must be obtained from several different areas.

The WCRO holds large collections of records from local hospitals, which could be of great interest in the study of women's history. Individual patients' records are probably the most rewarding area of study, but students should be aware that some of these records are closed for a hundred years; *bona fide* researchers, however, may apply for written permission to see them from the depositor. Central Hospital, Hatton (Warwick County Lunatic Asylum), is particularly well represented in these collections.[8]

Other local hospitals for which there are records are: Warneford, Leamington Spa[9], Rugby St Cross[10], Rugby St Luke[11],

Weston-under-Wetherley[12], and Middlefield Hospital, Knowle.[13]

There is a large holding for schools and other educational institutions at the WCRO. This covers school log books, managers' minutes, admission registers and Education Committee minutes, in which there may be material relevant to the education of girls. Researchers should look for details in the Schools Index. The General Index may also contain references to schools.

For a glimpse of women's lives during the nineteenth century, examination of the calendars and lists of prisoners and their depositions at Coventry, Warwick and Birmingham gaols can be rewarding. These are held in the Quarter Sessions Records; references are included in the Subject Index under 'Crime and Punishment'. There are also records for the prisoners in the House of Correction in Warwick, and their employment from 1828 to 1859.[14]

Quarter Sessions Records also list the numbers of prisoners in the Coventry House of Correction in 1816 - 18, with information of the money earned for heading pins, grinding corn and working in the worsted manufactory, including details of female prisoners.[15]

Quarter Sessions Order Books, the entry books of the Orders made by the Justices, detail many cases concerning women. Prominent among the subjects dealt with is the relief of the poor. Records exist for the years 1625 - 1773 (not continuous) and are in print in the County Record Series for 1625 - 1696 in the WCRO library.

Records of girls' reformatories are held at the WCRO: for example, Knowle Hill Community Home and Kenilworth.[16]

Almshouses are another type of institution in which women were involved. Accounts exist for Lady Katherine Leveson's Hospital at Temple Balsall.[17] The Parish Index contains details for other almshouses.

For information on women in workhouses, see the Poor Law section above.

PARISH RECORDS

These can include several different types of record such as the parish registers, Overseers' Accounts, Constables' Accounts and Churchwardens' Accounts.

In 1538 Thomas Cromwell decreed that parish registers should be kept to record marriages and deaths. A few registers do survive from this date, but 1558 is a more usual starting-point. During the Interregnum an Ordinance of 1664/5 laid down that birth dates should be noted in the parish records, and that parents' names and the dates of death and burial should be recorded. This was repealed at the Restoration but reinstated in 1663.

In 1754 the Hardwicke Marriage Act was passed to prevent clandestine marriages, and registers were printed. The Act of 1812 required the regulating and preservation of registers, and the format has changed very little. It is important to note that the registers record only the dates of baptism, marriage and burial. Banns are sometimes included in the parish registers.

The WCRO holds most of the Anglican parish records for Warwickshire. However, a few are still kept on the relevant church premises. Up to the twentieth century all registers are now on microfilm. The office also holds a few nonconformist and Roman Catholic registers on microfilm.[18] The Overseers' Accounts and Constables' Accounts may include information on arrests and dealings with female vagrants.[19]

QUARTER SESSIONS RECORDS

Quarter Sessions began in the Elizabethan period, but the WCRO holds records only from the 1620s. They fulfilled a legal and administrative rôle in the affairs of counties until their administrative rôle was taken over by County Councils in 1889, and their legal rôle was abolished in 1971. The court of Quarter Sessions filled a position

From the Powder Certificates for Curdworth, 1795

Warwickshire.
Hemlingford
Hundred.

BE it remembered, that on the 10th Day of September, 1762 the Persons, whose Names are here under written, came before Us, two of his Majesty's Justices of the Peace for the said County, and entered into Recognizance to our Sovereign Lord the King, as follows,

William Athins of Polesworth Weaver — in 10l. ⎫ Upon Condition.
John Fairfield of Do. Hatter — in 10 ⎭ Under-Written.

THE CONDITIONS of the above Recognizance are such, ~~the above Bounden~~ *Anne Harper of Polesworth Victualler* being licensed to keep a common Inn or Alehouse, where *she* now dwells, for one Year, from the 29th of this Instant. If the said *Anne Harper* shall keep good Order and Government, and suffer no unlawful Gaming in *her* House, Yard, Garden or Backside, nor wilfully offend against any other Act of Parliament now in Force for the Regulating of Victuallers, during the Term of *her* said License, then this Recognizance to be void or else to remain in full Force.

Taken and acknowledged, the ⎫
Day it bears Date, before Us. ⎭

Mendygate
J. Snoford

Victuallers' Recognisance for Anne Harper, 1762

Edward Holt ✗
Mary Gorman ✗
Ann Astley ✗   ⎫ Severally convicted of Felony — Ordered
Richard Oliver ✗ ⎬ to be removed from the said Gaol to
Elizabeth Allen ✗ ⎪ the said House of Correction there to be
William Greenhill ✗ ⎭ imprisoned for the space of 6 Calendar Months and kept to hard labour.

Richard Tate ✗   ⎫ Severally convicted of Felony — Ordered
Catherine Hughes ✗ ⎬ to be removed from the said Gaol to the said House of Correction there to be imprisoned for the space of 3 Calendar Months and kept to hard labour.

Richard Moulds ✗ Convicted of Fraud & Misdemeanor

Calender of Prisoners at Warwick House of Correction, 1801

between the Assize Court and the Petty Sessions. The Assize Court was presided over by circuit judges and tried the more serious cases. The courts of Quarter Sessions and the Petty Sessions were each administered by Justices of the Peace. Up to 1889 the Quarter Sessions acted as the main administrative body for the county, dealing with highways, bridges and the issuing of licences.

The Calendars of Prisoners list prisoners 'committed for felonies and misdemeanours' to Warwick gaol.[20] The name, age and offence are printed while the sentence or acquittal is handwritten. The House of Correction records list prisoners remaining in custody, and include many women. There are Depositions listing prisoners, their age, date of trial, offence, sentence and pressed charge, and include the individual deposition for each prisoner.[21] There are also Minute Books that detail offences and convictions, minutes of Sessions of 1674 - 1877 (printed 1625 - 1696) and records of Quarter Sessions, 1878 - 1970.[22] The book of 1789 - 1805 mentions women who are accused of vagrancy, assault, keeping disorderly houses, begging, being found 'wandering' in a parish, prostitution and being idle and disorderly persons. There are also Bastardy Orders from 1845.[23]

DIRECTORIES

These appeared in the last decades of the eighteenth century, but increased in number from the 1830s. They include useful topographical information on the county, arranged alphabetically by place-name, and list private residents, trades and professions. Some have advertisements. The WCRO holds some for the nineteenth century which include Spennell's and Beck's, available on microfilm, and also Pigot's and White's. They list many women who ran small businesses. Entries in White's Directory of 1850 advertise women in Leamington operating a bakery, a butcher's shop, a dairy and a haberdashery; they worked as laundresses, lodging-house keepers, milliners, dressmakers, teachers, stay and corset makers and straw hat makers.

> **MRS. SATCHWELL,**
> (Opposite the ruins) KENILWORTH.
>
> **TEA PARTIES ACCOMMODATED AT MODERATE CHARGES.**
>
> PARTIES ACCOMMODATED AT THE SHORTEST NOTICE.
> Ham, &c.   Tea Service and Hot Water supplied.

Mrs Satchwell's Tearoom; advertisement from White's Directory, 1874

RECORDS OF OLD-ESTABLISHED COUNTY FAMILIES

All counties have their aristocracy and gentry. The following is a selection from those who lived and owned property in Warwickshire, and the WCRO holds an extensive range of family collections.[24] The main collections include: Newdegate of Arbury,[25] Lucy of Charlecote,[26] Throckmorton of Coughton Court,[27] Shirley of Ettington,[28] Feilding of Newnham Paddox,[29] Seymour of Ragley Hall,[30] Mordaunt of Walton Hall[31] and Greville of Warwick Castle.[32]

References

1. These are listed in the RED TWINLOCK files containing the catalogues
2. CR 2017/C580/1 - 61
3. CR 1998/Box 60/Folder 1/1 - 6
4. CR 51
5. DR 126/687
6. These are listed in a black binder entitled *Newspapers at the CRO*, which is located on the shelves marked *General Lists*.
7. There are two separate blue folder lists. There is an index by surname to the 1851 census and for a number of parishes. These are found in separate maroon folders.
8. CR 1664, CR 2379, CR 2653 and CR 3162
9. CR 3068 and CR 2653/135
10. CR 2745
11. CR 3006
12. CR 3008
13. CR 2098
14. QS 24/593 - 6
15. QS 92/8 - 15
16. CR 2366
17. CR 112
18. Further information on these can be found in the reference section on the library shelves
19. See section on Poor Law
20. QS 26
21. QS 30
22. QS 39
23. QS 50
24. Although not every item is necessarily described in detail, it is worth reading through the *Catalogues of Archives Accessions* for references to women.
25. CR 136
26. L 6
27. CR 1988
28. CR 229
29. CR 2017
30. CR 114A
31. CR 1368
32. CR 1886

Warwickshire County Record Office Library

The WCRO library section holds many books relating to women; the following list gives a sample.

1. *Life's Ebb and Flow*, 1929, and *Afterthoughts*, 1931, by Frances, Countess of Warwick.[1]
   There are also two biographies written by Margaret Blunden and Theo Lang.

2. *The Cheverels of Cheverel Manor*, 1898, and *Gossip from a Muniment Room*, 1897, transcribed and edited by Lady Newdigate-Newdegate.[2]

3. *A Quest of Ladies - The Story of a Warwickshire School*, by Phyllis D. Hicks, an account of an early nineteenth-century school kept at Warwick, Barford and Stratford by Maria Byerley and her sisters.[3]

4. *She Dyed about Midnight*, 1992, by Jean Field, the history of Landor House including the establishment of King's High School, Warwick.[4]

5. *Marie Corelli; The Writer and the Woman*, 1903, by Thomas F.G. Coates and R.S. Warren Bell.[5]

6. *George Eliot's Life*, c. 1880, by J.W. Cross.[6]

7. *Mistress of Charlecote: The Memoirs of Mary Elizabeth Lucy*, 1983.[7]

8. *Mrs Milburn's Diaries*, 1979, edited by Peter Donnelly.[8]

9. *Old Q's Daughter*, 1951, by Bernard Falk, a biography of Maria Fagnani, the third Marchioness of Hertford.[9]

10. *Mary Rich, Countess of Warwick*, 1901, by C. Fell Smith.[10]

THESES

Apprenticeship in Warwickshire 1700 - 1834, by Joan Lane.[11]

Institutionalised Offenders - a study of the Victorian Institution and its inmates with special reference to late nineteenth-century Warwick, by Janet F. Saunders.[12]

Insanity and Private asylums in nineteenth-century Warwick, by Christine Liesenfeld.[13]

The Administration of the New Poor Law with particular reference to the Warwick Poor Law Union 1836 - 1863, by Peter Rex.[14]

RESEARCH NOTES

Coal-mining in Warwickshire, Teachers' Notes, Warwickshire Local History Group.[15]

REFERENCES

[1] C 920 GRE
[2] C 920 NEW
[3] C 376 Hic
[4] B WAR FIE
[5] C 920 COR
[6] C 920 ELI
[7] C 920 LUC
[8] C 920 MIL
[9] C 920 SEY
[10] C 920 RIC
[11] C 331 LAN
[12] C 362.2 SAU
[13] C 362.2 LIE
[14] C 362.5 REX
[15] C 622 WAR

Finding Women Through the Indexes

SUBJECT INDEX

This section is not a comprehensive coverage of the subject index; not every heading has been included. Examples have been selected to illustrate the variety and wealth of information available at the WCRO.

ACCOUNTS

This section includes household bills, estate accounts, bills and vouchers, receipts, bank and cash books, executors' accounts, housekeepers' accounts and charities. Among the many references to women are the accounts for carpenters' work, *c.* 1600, belonging to Mrs Holbach,[1] the personal accounts in 1786 and 1818 of Miss Ann Grove, and the personal and business accounts of Elizabeth S. and Ellen Landor of 1829 to 1854 and 1855.[2]

The Marquess of Hertford's servants' wages bill of 1797 to 1805 shows the women servants' positions and wages, and there is evidence that the Marquess employed a female clock-cleaner.[3]

The Wages Book of the Lady Leveson Hospital at Temple Balsall for 1819 to 1841 has entries for female nurses, under-nurses, housemaids and cooks.[4]

AUSTRALIA

Although in the eighteenth century many people were transported to Australia, in the nineteenth century thousands emigrated to take advantage of the great opportunities offered there. Some verses were addressed to Ellen Burgess on her departure for Australia in 1848.[5]

A page from Lady Anne Newdegate's household accounts, 1600

NOTICE

TO

YOUNG WOMEN

DESIROUS OF BETTERING THEIR CONDITION BY AN

Emigration to New South Wales.

In New South Wales and Van Diemen's Land there are very few Women compared with the whole number of People, so that it is impossible to get Women enough as Female Servants or for other Female Employments. The consequence is, that desirable situations, with good wages, are easily obtained by Females in those Countries; but the Passage is so long that few can pay the expence of it without help. There is now, however, the following favourable opportunity of going to New South Wales.

The Committee of a Charitable Society in London, called the Refuge for the Destitute, intends to send out a Ship in the course of the Spring, expressly for the conveyance of Female Emigrants. The Parties who go in that Vessel must be *Unmarried Women or Widows;* must be *between the Ages of* 18 *and* 30; and must be of *good health and character*. They must also *be able to pay* £6 towards the expense of their Passage. The remainder of the expense will be paid by the Society. Every arrangement will be made for the comfort of the Emigrants during the Voyage; they will be taken care of on their first landing in the Colonies; and they will find there, ready for them, a list of the different situations to be obtained, and of the wages offered, so that they may at once see the different opportunities of placing themselves. The Women sent out in this manner will not be bound to any person whatsoever, but will be, to all intents and purposes, Free Women.

Persons who on reading this Notice, may desire to emigrate in the manner pointed out, should apply by Letter to the "Secretary to the Refuge for the Destitute, Hackney Road, London." If the Letter be sent by General Post, it should be sent under a cover addressed to "The Under Secretary of State, Colonial Department, London." It will be proper that the Application should be accompanied by recommendations from the Resident Minister of the Parish, and from any other respectable persons to whom the Applicant may be known; the same recommendations should state the fact that the Applicant will be able to pay £6. when she shall receive notice that it is time to embark.

All Applications made in the foregoing manner, will receive early Answers.

Parties who may be desirous to obtain information by personal application in the City, may have all further particulars from Mr. John Marshall, 26, Birchin Lane, Cornhill.

(Signed)   EDWARD FORSTER,
CHAIRMAN.

Refuge for the Destitute,
Hackney Road, London,
19th January, 1833.

By Authority.—J. Hartnell, Fleet-street, London.

A Notice to young women about emigration to New South Wales, 1833

There is a copy of a printed notice to young women desirous of bettering their condition by emigration to New South Wales, issued by the Emigration Committee in 1833.[6]

BASTARDY

These include lists of bastardy cases brought to Quarter Sessions between 1773 and 1835, and also bastardy applications between 1881 and 1915, and 1924.[7]

CHARITIES

There were hundreds of local charities that gave assistance to those in need. These included lying-in charities for mothers in childbirth, for example, Warwick Lying-In Charity. The rules from the late nineteenth century and the scheme of 1974 are deposited here.[8]

There were also educational charities, and some for apprentices and poor widows. There are records detailing donations made by women, and some charities were established by benefactresses: for example, Ann Johnson's Charity in Warwick from 1596 to 1888, and Sarah Greville's Charity for Knowle and Warwick, for which the WCRO holds accounts from 1720 to 1855.[9]

COMMONPLACE BOOKS

These were personal notebooks which became popular in the eighteenth century. Maria Crynes's book of 1758 is an example of beautiful handwriting. She copied out items that interested her, for example, a letter from Mr Pope to Mr Cromwell, and she also included some classical correspondence. In a letter from Laura to Aurelia, Laura described how she hated the country and that 'daylight makes me sick; it has something in it so common and vulgar', and in a rhyming couplet complained:

> 'Green Fields and shady Groves and crystal Springs
> And Larks and Nightingales are odious things.'[10]

Lady Horatia Waldegrave's book written between 1775 and 1779 included verses by Horace Walpole written at Strawberry Hill on 15 August 1779 to the Marchioness of Blandford. Another poem by Walpole written in 1772 or 1773 was on the three Misses Vernon, one of whom married the Earl of Warwick in 1776.[11]

CRIME AND PUNISHMENT

An execution poster of Mary Ball, in 1849 commemorates the last public execution in Coventry. The poster includes verses and an account of the trial and execution.[12]

The Known Thieves Album *c.* 1895 to 1910 contains photographs, physical descriptions and a record of convictions of about 1400 people, kept probably in the Aston Division of the County Constabulary. There are at least a dozen pages of female criminals. Their crimes are listed and their appearance is a good source of social history, particularly for costume and hairstyles.[13]

A fraud case in 1861 concerned Catherine Barbara Wilson, wife of Captain William le Hunte Wilson, who was trying to pass off her son as her husband's child.[14]

There are also letters referring to a visit from prison reformer, Elizabeth Fry, in the late eighteenth century.[15]

Execution Poster, 1849, for Mary Ball, the last person to be publicly executed in Coventry

Fashion Plate from Francis Sneyd's Pocket Book, 1768

DEATH

There are a few funeral accounts for women in this section, one of which is for Mary Perman, possibly late seventeenth century.[16] Also included are Registers of Deaths in Warwick Union Workhouse from 1848 to 1914.[17] There is a Stay of Execution for Ann Eatwell, who had been sentenced for the murder of her new-born child in 1863.[18]

DIARIES

The WCRO holds large numbers of diaries, some of which make very varied reading. Four examples are: Lady Templeton (two volumes) between 1897 and 1906;[19] Charlotte Newdigate, 1860;[20] Caroline Carey's journal of her tour in Europe in 1855 and 1857;[21] and Georgiana S. Miller of Radway, from 1851 to 1900.[22]

Sarah Warriner, who lived from 1792 until 1860, writing in 1805 in her pocket book, *The London Fashionable and Polite Repository*, mentions *Lovers' Vows*, the play rehearsed in Jane Austen's *Mansfield Park*. She includes a cutting from a newspaper advertising for a wife.[23]

In Frances Sneyd's pocketbooks or diaries, there are a number of tiny late eighteenth- and early nineteenth-century fashion plates. In 1803 she went to Bath and listed what she paid for dress materials and accessories, including a white feather, a tippet, black lace, ribbons, beads, and some velvet and washballs.[24]

Eleanor Archer's diaries are very detailed, containing such items as recipes, lace-making and knitting patterns and advice on how to live a 'moral' life.[25]

Fashion Plate from Francis Sneyd's Pocket Book, 1801

Clapham Terrace School, Leamington Spa, 1902

EDUCATION

This section has a huge number of entries covering a wide variety of areas, from bills for children's schooling to material about teachers. Among the many documents are bills and accounts for the education of Mary Tomes at Worcester and Leamington *c*.1807-21[26], and Annette Farr's exercise book (writing) in 1826.[27]

An unnamed schoolgirl, who lived in either Wixford or Bidford and went to school in Leicester, wrote her diary in *The Ladies Complete Pocket Book*. The diary was written in 1797 and contains tables for cashing wages and an index for holidays and 'remarkable' days. In part IV of the pocket book, the diarist was kept up to date with a 'Variety of New Songs, Country Dances, Rebus and Enigmas'.

She noted that she 'Received 12d on a wig in one half year (June) of Mrs Hefford and much fruit 11d. Miss Simpson bought Muslin at 4/8d and ribbon 1d'. Her personal comments are often enigmatic; 'Miss Wilson was married to Mr Wood on Thursday 22 September 1796. They set of *[sic]* for Birmingham to stay a week. I think Miss Wilson is very unhappy'. 'George Davenport was hanged on Monday August 29 1797. We saw him go by in his shroud'.

The events she recorded often concern food. She went frequently to drink tea and received gifts of food from her uncle 'some plumb puding *[sic]* and two chees *[sic]* cakes and a paper of sweetmeets'.

In a printed essay, 'Advice to Ladies', the writer argues that education relevant to a person's status in life is essential, but that all ladies should understand housekeeping. The writer is highly critical of boarding schools, labelling them 'seminaries of vice and nurseries of idleness and extravagance'.[28]

In a handwritten notebook belonging to Barbara Maria Legge dated 29 October 1808, she argues for further education for girls. In particular, she is adamant that reading is the most important activity to assist in 'forming the mind, cultivating the taste and fixing the principles'. The learning of a foreign language was an accomplishment; however, reading and understanding it well enough to go beyond the words would enable the pupil to grasp new ideas and broaden the mind. If books were discussed with a parent or friend their value would be doubled. As a result, young ladies would think for themselves and discriminate between false and true knowledge.[29]

FOOD

Among the many recipe books in the WCRO a large vellum-covered book belonging to Mary Wise contains dozens of medical and culinary recipes from the eighteenth century. Instructions for making cosmetics such as 'lipsave' *(sic)* and 'Pomatum for the face' are jumbled up with remedies for plague and mad dog bites, and cookery recipes. After including 'A Most Excellent Medicine against the Plague', the following lines suggest the horror still occasioned by outbreaks of such epidemics:

> Keep this as your Life above all things in the plague time under God trust to this there never was Man Woman or Child that it deceived tis good also in the Smallpox Measels Surfeits or fevers.

The ingredients reflect the ancient knowledge of herbal medicine and use of electuaries (a medical conserve or paste, consisting of a powder or other ingredients mixed with honey, preserves or syrup of some kind). Tin and quicksilver were suggested as ingredients in cures for worms and pewter was included in salves.[30]

There are numbers of other recipe books, among them those of: Lady Templetown, *c*.1800;[31] Ann Greswold of Hillfield Hall, Solihull;[32] Jessie Holbeche (1913-1918);[33] Sarah Warriner, 1813-57;[34] Catherine Collins, mid-nineteenth century[35] and Kitty Robinson, late nineteenth century.[36] These books are not confined to culinary matters, but include remedies for ailments and diseases.

Tunbridge Cakes / 106 Take 2 pound of Flower a pound of butter & a quat of a pound of Sugar almost a pint of Milk, 1 Egg an Ounce of Caraway Seeds mix your Seeds & Sugar with your Flower then rub in your butter to make it into a limber paste Role it very thin & lay them on a tin plate & bake them till they are a little coloured you may make them broad or long as you please

To Make Calfs Feet Jelly / 107 Take 2 good Calfs Feet & put them into a Clean pot cutting them into peices, & put to them 4 Quarts of Water covering them very close, put an Ounce of hartshorne & an Ounce of Ivory into it, letting them boil very well till they come to 2 Quarts, then Strain them & put them into a Clean pan, & let it stand till it is thorough Cold, to take of all the fat, then put it into the pot again till it is all melted, then take it from of the fire again, that it may not be to hot, & have 8 Whites of Eggs well beaten, & put into the pot of Jelly, & ½ a pound of treble refin'd Sugar, & a pint of Rhenish & a quarter of a pint of Sack, the juice of 4 large Lemons & the peeles of 2 Lemons must be put into it, let all these be boyled a quarter of an hour but do not Stir the Jelly when boiling nor afterward, only take it up in a Cup, & put it into a Bag & throw it up often till it is Clear to keep in Glasses. If made in the Summer you must add one Calfs foot more

To Make a Pudding of whole Rice / 108 Take ½ a pound of whole Rice & 3 pints of Milk, & pick the Rice clean, & put it into the Milk, & boil it tender & the Milk almost boyl'd away, then Stir in ½ a pound butter & ½ a pound of Sugar & let it boyl a little together & you must put into it the quantity of a Nutmeg in mace finely beaten, this is a very good plain pudding, but if you have a mind to it you may put into it after it is of from the fire & allmost Cold 4 Yolks of Eggs stirring it very well together

A page from Mary Wise's recipe book, no date

HOSPITALS

Included in the many references are minutes and reports, and registers of admissions and discharges, for a number of local hospitals. This heading covers isolation hospitals, homes for incurables and infirmaries. Some of these records provide information on both patients and staff. Researchers should be aware that some of these records are closed for one hundred years, but *bona fide* researchers may apply to the depositor for written permission to see them. There are references to nursing in the Poor Law material.

INSANITY

There were several asylums for the treatment of the mentally ill in Warwickshire, the main establishment being the Central Hospital at Hatton. The WCRO holds a large collection of records, the clinical ones available only after one hundred years, in accordance with the Public Records Acts.[37]

The WCRO holds many documents up to 1895 that illustrate the development of attitudes towards the treatment of mental illness. A study of women's casenotes reveals contemporary perceptions of disease; to a modern reader it may seem that observers did not distinguish between physical and mental conditions. Psychiatry was in its infancy, and few remedies existed beyond care and attention. Female nursing and domestic staff wages records from 1936 to 1946 and some staff records from 1874 to 1899 are available.[38]

The insane continued to be cared for in workhouses, and some of their records are deposited. Three examples are the Alcester Union,[39] the Warwick Union[40] and the Birmingham Workhouse.[41] The index refers to many individual case records, especially those of women.

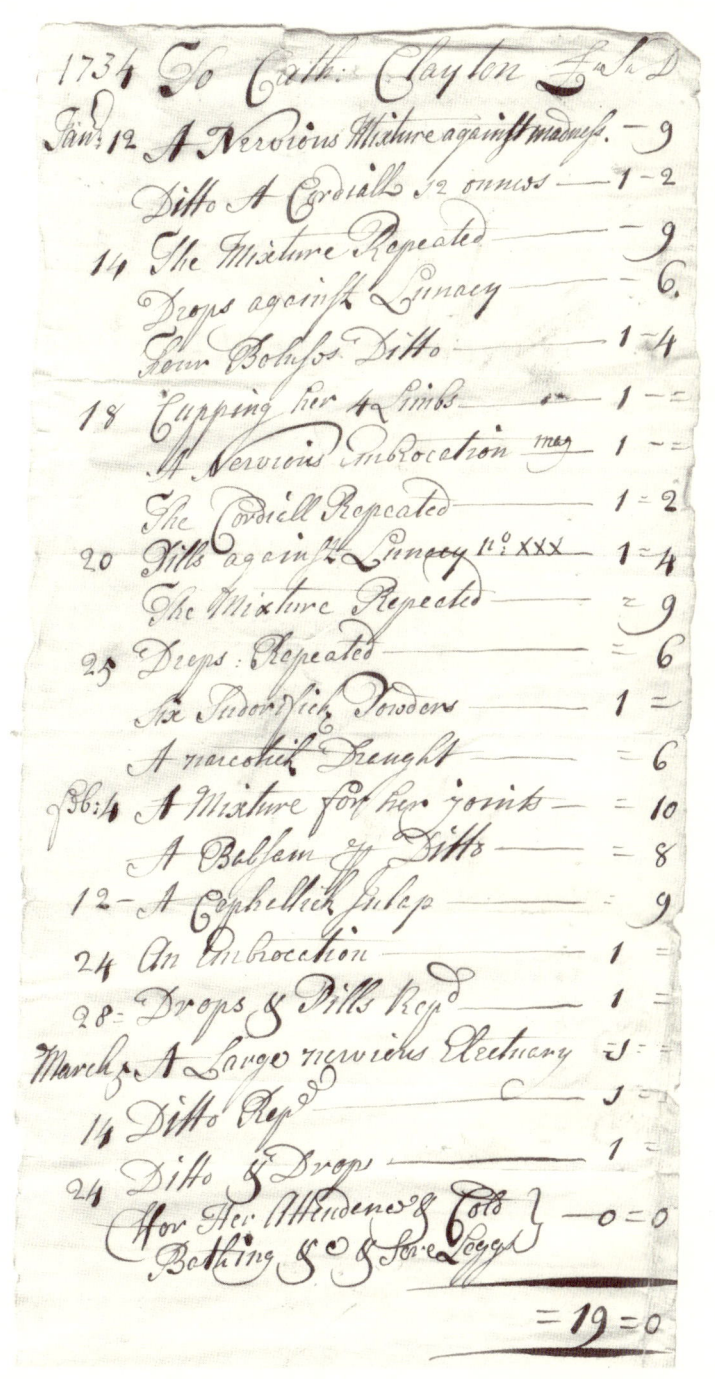

		£	s	d
1734	To Cath: Clayton			
Jan: 12	A Nervious Mixture against madness		—	9
	Ditto A Cordiall 12 ounces		1	2
14	The Mixture Repeated		—	9
	Drops against Lunacy		—	6
	Four Bolus's Ditto		1	4
18	Cupping her 4 Limbs		1	—
	A Nervious Embrocation may		1	—
	The Cordiell Repeated		1	2
20	Pills against Lunacy No XXX		1	4
	The Mixture Repeted		—	9
25	Drops: Repeated		—	6
	Six Sudorifick Powders		1	—
	A narcotick Draught		—	6
Feb: 4	A Mixture for her joints		—	10
	A Balsam &c Ditto		—	8
12	A Cephellick Julep		—	9
24	An Embrocation		1	—
28	Drops & Pills Repd		1	—
March 7	A Large nervious Electuary		5	—
14	Ditto Repd		5	—
24	Ditto & Drops		1	—
	For her Attendence & Cold Bathing &c & Sore Leggs	0	0	0
		= 19	=	0

A list of medicines administered to Catherine Clayton for insanity in the workhouse, Shipston-on-Stour, 1734

Warwick Laundry, 1930

LABOUR

Many varied types of documents are included in this section. There is no direct reference to women, but obviously there were, for example, female apprenticeships. Women would also be mentioned in indentures, charities accounts and registers, which come under this heading.

During the nineteenth century women's occupations were largely ignored, so it is therefore exciting to find in the Newdegate of Arbury Collection a Garden Labour Book that records women employed in weeding, sweeping, carrying pots, spreading dung and earth, hay-making, bee-keeping, snail-gathering and slipping strawberries.[42] There are many wages books relating to staff, servants and labourers. These cover landed estates, firms, businesses and institutions and range over a considerable period. Young persons from the workhouse sent out as servants were listed in registers, some of which have been deposited.

In this section, among papers relating to Eleanor Archer, there is a volume containing specimen advertisements for occupations for professional women *c.* 1900.[43]

LIBRARIES

This index includes lists of books belonging to many Warwickshire people, and knowledge of a woman's reading material can often give perspectives into her personality. Several women are mentioned, for example Juliana Newdegate,[44] a seventeenth-century member of the Arbury family. Another member of the family, Lady Mary Newdegate,[45] also owned many books, and some belonging to Miss Landor, *c.* 1880, a descendant of the poet Walter Savage Landor of Warwick, are also listed.[46]

MARRIAGE

There is a wide variety of entries, making this section particularly rewarding. When John J. Murcott of Whitnash advertised for a wife in 1884 and 1887 eighteen women replied.[47] Many of the letters came from women in service, and illustrate a good level of literacy; they are moving documents and reflect the women's desperation.

There are many separation agreements, a bigamy case,[48] and Jane Hitchcock's affidavit of good character of 1581 on her marriage to a minister.[49]

The WCRO holds diaries of marriages at the Court House, Warwick, in 1945 and 1946.[50]

There is a document listing reasons why one of the brethren of the Lord Leycester Hospital, Warwick, in 1817 should not marry a young wife.[51]

Finally, there is an eighteenth-century love letter to a Miss Jenny (although the writer is contracted to marry another), and an early eighteenth-century 'Wedding Song' from a bridegroom to Maria, his bride.[52]

MEDICINE

This can be found under a number of sub-headings, which are listed in the Index. The Eleanor Archer collection contains the Viavi Gynaecological Plates, which were designed in 1891 to educate women on the diseases of the uterine organs.[53]

There are twentieth-century records deposited by Warwickshire County Council on its Maternity and Child Welfare Committees and other documents on midwives and health visitors. An interesting apprenticeship indenture of 1803 concerns a male midwife.[54]

The casebook of Thomas W. Jones, surgeon of Henley-in-Arden, records the midwifery cases in Henley and the Wootton Wawen area from 1780 to 1800; these include some lecture notes.[55]

Under the sub-heading 'Maternity' is a set of rules for the late nineteenth-century Warwick Lying-in Charity.[56]

Under the sub-heading 'Drugs' there is an account of the tragic death of Charlotte G. Lewis from the excessive use of laudanum and ardent spirits in the early nineteenth century.[57]

Two examples of cross-referencing are Lady Templetown's recipe collection c. 1800 and Sarah Warriner's of Bloxham Grove.[58]

NONCONFORMITY

Aspects of women's lives in a religious context are disclosed in the correspondence of the Quaker family, Lowe of Ettington.[59] The collection contains letters received by Jeffrey Bevington Lowe, who lived from 1774 to 1864, from his brothers and his sisters, Anna, Deborah and Elizabeth. They and their spouses were writing between 1803 and 1849, and their letters illustrate women's participation in religious activities. Of particular interest are about forty-five letters from Anna.

The letters are beautifully written, at a gentle pace, and contain nothing dramatic or exciting. The general tenor is reflective, redolent of the Quaker way of life. It is interesting to note how many times people were 'ill', 'unwell' or 'poorly'. Their brother, John, suffered from delicate health. Every letter starts with an apology for the length of time elapsed since they last corresponded with each other. Despite the often very formal tone of these letters, it is clear that the Lowe family tie was particularly strong and loving. The Quaker religion clearly provided all family members with a very deep faith that permeated all aspects of their lives, in both a social and a business sense.

Other Quaker records in the twentieth century indicate women's participation in the movement. Minute and account books are clinical and factual, but women's activities can be gleaned from careful study. One example is the Minute Book of the Rugby Society of Friends,[60] which covered the years from January 1920 to December 1936. Gertrude Sugden is first mentioned on 11 January 1920, when she was proposed as Representative to Monthly Meetings. She was appointed to this post in February, and also to be a representative to the Women's Monthly Meetings. She became more involved and was appointed Librarian in March 1928, authorised to 'purchase a selection of Tracts for the box'. In July she went with three male colleagues to Monthly Meetings in Birmingham. As a result of discussions on Reconstituted Famine Corn, she consented to be appointed to the Monthly Meetings.

The minutes of 8 October record that Gertrude Sugden has been asked to report on finances at the recent quarterly meeting. In November 1921 the clerk retired, and she was appointed in his place. She was now writing and signing minutes. She continued as Clerk until 1927, when she resigned because she was leaving the district.

NURSING

An alternative to the use of a wet nurse is referred to in a document of 1827, describing the feeding of a small baby 'with victuals taken through a parchment tied to a vessel for the purpose'.[61]

There is a volume containing lectures on midwifery and details of 422 deliveries.[62]

A large number of records of many District Nursing Associations is held by the WCRO.

Hampstead 2/4 mo 1817

My dear Brother,

My C C & myself having been from home more than a week attending our Quarterly Meetg &c, we did not until yesterday get the account of our dear & valuable Grandfather's removal from this state of mutability, & my sister Deb's writing hastily gave us few particulars — such a circumstance was so entirely unanticipated by us that it really introduced our minds into a more than common degree of painful feeling, & had we suffered any suitable opportunity to have passed over, whereby we might have once more enjoyed a personal interview, I believe our regret would have been deep. This however is not the case, & tho' a knowledge of his illness, had it been sufficiently long, for our obtaining it, would I believe have induced us to have used every endeavour for seeing him before his departure — we are best satisfied to make an effort for paying the last tribute of affection to the dear remains I accordingly think of leaving Uxbridge tomorrow morg in an Oxford coach accompanied by my sister Deb. & taking Chaise's thence to Catyngton, where I hope we may

Part of a letter to the Quaker, Jeffery Bevington Lowe,
from his sister, Anne, 1817

PERSONAL PAPERS

Although this is not a large section, it contains several documents concerning women. There are examples of women's wills and inventories[63] and many references to marriage agreements and settlements.[64] The fortune settled on Mary Lewis, née Greswolde, at the time of her marriage to David Lewis of Cardigan, is documented in the collection, which covers the years from 1711 to 1712.[65]

REGISTRATION, CIVIL

From July 1837 the registration of births, marriages and deaths commenced. There is an indictment for failure to register a birth in 1838.[66] There are registers of births in Warwick Union Workhouse from 1848 to 1914.[67]

TEXTILES

Not all documents are written; there is a collection of photographs of bed-hangings and covers embroidered by members of the Warwickshire Federation of WIs and presented to Lady Ilkeston in 1927.[68]

A contract for employment was drawn up between a female staymaker and Eliza and Martha Lloyd, milliners of Leamington, in 1829, at £30 per annum.[69]

One of two bills belonging to a Miss Pemberton in 1806 discloses the vast sum of £6 18s 8d spent at a Birmingham drapers on lace. The previous day she had spent 17s 6d on a similar purchase. The two letterheads are elaborately designed and decorative.[70]

Women barrowing coke at a gas works during the First World War

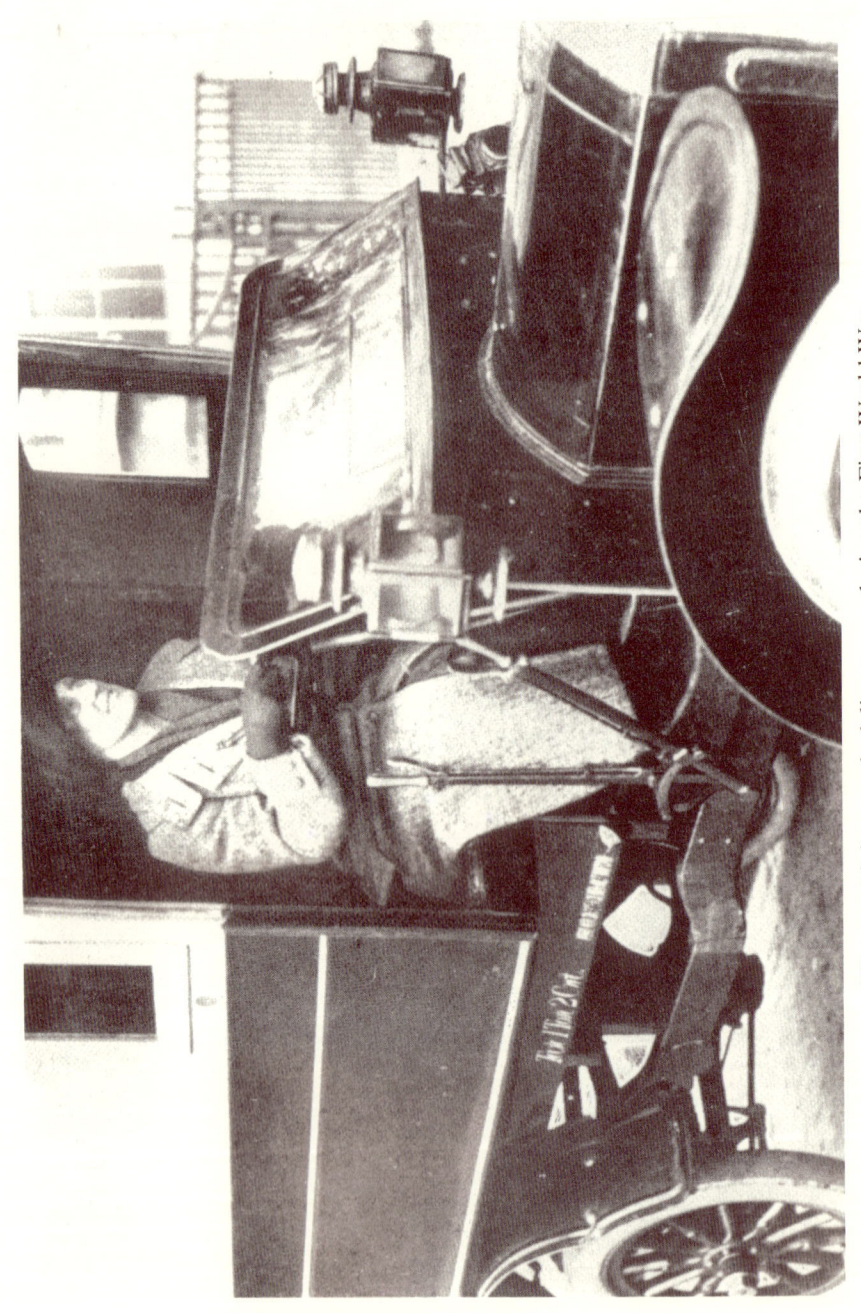

Woman driving goods delivery van during the First World War

Women brewery workers during the First World War

WAR

Men and women on active service from 1943 to 1945 are listed for the Alcester area.[71] Miss Norah Slater compiled some notes on life in Warwick during the Second World War.[72]

Women's War Work was a booklet issued by the War Office in 1916. It contains many photographs depicting the wide variety of jobs undertaken by women during this period, ranging from window-cleaning and driving steam rollers to making shells and motor cycles.[73]

WELFARE

This is a very large section, but there is little specific reference to women. However, it includes much detailed information on workhouses, the administration of the Poor Law, settlement documents and many overseers' accounts.[74]

WOMEN

This is the section in which students would hope to find the bulk of documents concerning women. Although it is not very large, there is a variety of items that reward the researcher. An eighteenth-century mother's instructions to her household on the care of her daughter reveal that family feelings were as relevant then as today.[75]

Deposits include documents on the First World War land-workers.[76]

There is extensive material on the activities of the Warwickshire Women's Institutes; there are also records of Kenilworth Female Friendly Society between 1826 and 1987.[77]

Women window cleaners during the First World War

AN EIGHTEENTH CENTURY MOTHER'S INSTRUCTIONS TO HER HOUSEHOLD

¶ As I look upon it to be the first Duty of every Mother to form the disposition of her child, and as my endeavours will not succeed to my wish unless everybody in the house acts agreeably to the rules I have laid down, you are requested to observe the following towards my daughter:

¶ Never to speak to her in a manner you would not chuse she should speak to you when she is grown up.

¶ Always to treat her with kindness and tenderness, but not with flattery or dependance; not to pay any court to her as to a superior, lest she should become proud; but to pay her what attention her weak state, incapable of helping itself, demands—let her understand, as soon as she is capable, it is on that account.

¶ Never to deceive her, or use any deceit before her, on any account whatever; nor to let any appearance of deceit or falsehood in her go unnoticed, but mention it to *her* at the moment, and inform *me* of it afterwards.

¶ Never to let her ask twice for what it is not improper for her to have; nor ever to let her have what is improper because she may want it; and never to give her a thing you have at first denied because she begs or cries for it.

¶ If she has got anything at any time which it is not proper for her to have, not to snatch it away from her in a hurry, or take it by force, but coolly and steadily make her give it you.

¶ If at any time she puts herself in a passion, not to endeavour to coax and to sooth her, but to set her down and take no further notice of her, but, now and then asking her if she is good, and when she says she is, then to caress her and wipe up her tears.

¶ If she is obstinate and will not do anything that she is desired, if you have once made a point of it, not to give it up, but stand firmly but mildly to it till it is done.

¶ Upon no consideration whatever to say or do anything that may frighten her, such as threatening to put her in the dark, or alone, or that anything will come and run away with her if she is not good, or the like.

¶ If she has been corrected in the parlour, not to indulge and make much of her when she comes out, but treat her with the same coolness we do till she is forgiven, nor ever say that it was hard or cruel to use her so, as she will never be punish'd without a necessity, and then the more solemn it is made the seldomer it will be wanted.

PRINTED BY CASSELL & COMPANY, LIMITED, LA BELLE SAUVAGE, LONDON, E.C.

62

An eighteenth-century mother's instructions to her household concerning her daughter

The Suffragette march in Stratford-upon-Avon on the way to London on 16 July 1913

RULES

TO BE OBSERVED

BY A

SOCIETY OF WOMEN,

IN THE PARISH OF

KENILWORTH.

Commencing in JUNE, 1798.

Coventry:

PRINTED BY N. ROLLASON, IN HIGH-STREET.

RULES, &c.

IT being usual for men to form themselves into clubs, for their support, under sickness and misfortunes, there seems to be no reason why women who are exposed to equal if, not greater sufferings, should not unite for the same good purpose, and from their own honest industry lay by a trifle for the hour of need. It is proposed, therefore, that the women of this parish do form themselves into a club, and that this institution be carried on in a peaceable and friendly manner, subject to the following rules;

I.

THAT the club be governed by two patronesses and two stewards.

II. THAT one of the stewards be chosen by the patronesses, and the other by a majority of the club every six months.

III. ANY member refusing to act as steward shall forfeit *two shillings* and *six-pence*: any steward absent at the monthly meeting shall for-

From the Book of Rules of the Society of Women, Kenilworth, 1798

This Indenture, made the _Third_ — Day of _August_ — in the _Fifty Third_ Year of the Reign of our Sovereign Lord GEORGE the _Third_ — by the Grace of GOD, of the United Kingdom of Great-Britain and Ireland, King, Defender of the Faith, and in the Year of our Lord One Thousand Eight Hundred and _Thirteen_ **Witnesseth,** that _James Monro_ — and _John King_ Churchwardens, of the _Parish_ — of _Nuneaton_ in the County of _Warwick_ — and _Thomas Adcock_ — — — — — by and with the Consent of His Majesty's Justices of the Peace for the said County, whose Names are hereunto subscribed, have put and placed, and by these Presents do put and place, _Maria Harrison_ — — — — — — — Years or thereabouts, a poor Child, of the said _Parish_ Apprentice to _Thomas Harrison of the Parish of Nuneaton in the County of Warwick Ribbon Weaver_ _____ with _him_ to dwell and serve, from the Day of the Date of these Presents, until the said Apprentice shall accomplish _her_ full Age of _Twenty one Years_ according to the Statute in that Case made and provided ; during all which Term, the said Apprentice _her_ said M_aster_ faithfully shall serve in all lawful Businesses, according to _her_ Power, Wit, and Ability ; and honestly, orderly and obediently in all Things demean and behave _her_self towards _her_ said M_aster_ and all _his_ during the said Term : And the said _Thomas Harrison_ for _him_self — _his_ Executors and Administrat_ors_, doth covenant and grant to and with the said Churchwardens and Overseers and every of them, their's and every of their Executors and Administrators, and their's and every of their Successors, for the Time being, by these Presents, that _he_ the said _Thomas Harrison_ _his Master_ shall and will teach and instruct, or cause to be taught and instructed, in the best Way and Manner that _he_ can : And shall and will, during all the Term aforesaid, find, provide, and allow unto the said Apprentice competent and sufficient Meat, Drink, Apparel, Lodging, Washing, and other Things necessary and fit for an Apprentice : **Provided always,** that the said lastmentioned Covenant, on the Part and Behalf of the said _Thomas Harrison_ h_is_ Executors and Administrators, to be done and performed, shall continue and be in Force for no longer Time than Three Calendar Months next after the Death of the said _Thomas Harrison_ _____ in Case the said _Thomas Harrison_ _____ shall happen to die during the Continuance of such Apprenticeship, according to the Provisions of an Act, passed in the Thirty-Second Year of the Reign of King GEORGE the Third, intituled, " An " Act for the further Regulation of Parish Apprentices :". And also shall and will so provide for the said Apprentice, that _she_ will save the said _Parish_ _____ or Parishioners of the same, but of and from all Charge shall and be not any Ways a Charge to the said _Parish_ _____ and Parishioners harmless and indemnified during the said Term.

WE whose Names are here underwritten, Justices of the Peace for the said _County_ (whereof one is of the Quorum) do consent to the Putting forth _Maria Harrison_ _____ an Apprentice, according to the Intent and Meaning of this Indenture.

Sealed and delivered in the Presence of

In Witness whereof the Parties above-said to these present Indentures interchangeably have set their Hands and Seals, the Day and Year first above written.

Eleven-year-old Maria Harrison's apprenticeship indenture as a ribbon weaver, 1813.

APPRENTICESHIP INDEXES

Records exist about the lives of many working women and young girls. The WCRO holds only the Warwick, Nuneaton and Coleshill Parish Apprenticeship Registers. However, there are many apprenticeship records, especially indentures, from the seventeenth century, in parish and overseers' accounts. Many girls were apprenticed into some decent trades, especially in the eighteenth century, and some charities were exclusively for girls, giving them a better start in a more rewarding career than the parish could. In the Nuneaton Apprenticeship Index for the late eighteenth and early nineteenth centuries, cotton-spinning and ribbon-weaving are major occupations for girls of ten and twelve. In 1801, Sarah Affleck is listed as being a ribbon-weaver, aged nine. Hannah Arnol and Mary Baily, both aged thirteen, were apprenticed in 1815. According to the Warwick Apprenticeship Index, girls carried out a variety of tasks in the textile industry such as thread-making, silk-throwing and ribbon-weaving. The Coleshill Apprenticeship Index indicates a range of occupations including cotton-weaving, housewifery, button-burnishing, ribbon-weaving and mantua-making.

PHOTOGRAPHIC INDEX

There are fairly comprehensive indexes by Place and Subject, and a very incomplete one of Persons. A search through the Subject Index can be rewarding; for example, under 'Laundries' there is a photograph of women at work in Warwick Steam Laundry in about 1930.[78]

Under 'Suffragettes' a Suffrage march through Stratford-upon-Avon in 1913 is recorded.[79]

Under 'Tennis' in this section, there is a photograph of King's High School girls dressed for a game in 1918.[80]

In the 'Persons' section there is a portrait of Eleanor Doorly, who was headmistress of the King's High School, Warwick, from 1922 to 1944.[81]

WILLS INDEX

This is arranged by surname. The WCRO is not a probate office; however, there are some women's wills among those deposited. The following is a random selection.

In a copy of a will dated 17 July 1711, Jane Davis of Solihull, spinster, leaves a fourth part of a house called the Pinfold in Solihull and lands going with it to Roger Paine of Budbrooke, whom she intends to marry if she recovers, in trust to pay legacies to her three sisters, Mary, Margaret and Martha.[82]

A Probate document dated 1678 of Rose Cattell, spinster of Warwick, is deposited with an inventory, legacy receipts and two deeds covering the years 1633 to 1682.[83]

GENERAL INDEX

This is arranged by place name and the surnames of important families.

PERSONAL NAMES INDEX

There are two indexes, pre-1535 and post-1535. Each is arranged by surname, and neither is complete. They may not be particularly helpful, as the references are mainly to parties or witnesses in title deeds.

PROPERTY INDEX

This index contains references to small collections of documents relating to individual places.

REFERENCES

1. CR 1618/W15/9
2. CR 162/641, CR 1908/281, 283, 284 - 5, 286 - 8
3. CR 114A/222/7/1, CR 114A/222/18/167
4. CR 112/Bal79
5. CR 1680/28
6. DR 583/98
7. CR 1741/1, CR 2715/17
8. Z 832(sm)
9. CR 1618/WA6/113 - 154, CR 1618/WA17/96 - 7, CR 1282/1, CR170/382 - 454
10. CR 544/312
11. CR 114A/537/1
12. C 343 Lif(L)(p)
13. CR 2212
14. CR 71/105
15. CR 1534
16. CR 1334/84/1 - 12
17. CR 51/1695 - 98
18. Z 831(sm)
19. CR 426
20. CR 136/A539
21. CR 1374/7
22. CR 1382/3 - 8
23. CR 1635/56
24. CR 136/A554 - 559
25. CR 367/1 - 9
26. CR 1470/Bundle 7
27. CR 3087/3
28. CR 1704
29. CR 136/A566
30. CR 341/301

[31] CR 426/Box 1
[32] CR 1291/458
[33] CR 1680/102
[34] CR 1635/66, 67
[35] CR 2025/2
[36] CR 2775/1
[37] CR 1664
[38] CR 1664/148, 149
[39] CR 51/88
[40] CR 51/1762
[41] QS 111/106
[42] CR 1841/59
[43] CR 2025/3
[44] CR 136/B6
[45] CR 136/B576
[46] CR 1908/323
[47] CR 556/508, 510
[48] DR 126/719/16
[49] Z 245(SM)
[50] CR 1618/W26
[51] CR 1600/53/5,6
[52] Z 656/12 - 13 (sm.)
[53] CR 367/44 - 45
[54] CR 890/16
[55] CR 3019 & Z 383 (sm.)
[56] Z 832(sm)
[57] CR 1291/437
[58] These may also be found under FOOD.
[59] CR 2926/1-78
[60] CR 2208/2
[61] CR 2926/61
[62] Z 383(sm)
[63] CR 299/655/1 - 24
[64] CR 229/662/1 - 4
[65] CR 299/611/1 - 8
[66] QS 5/73
[67] CR 51/1693 - 1694
[68] CR 367/129/70
[69] CR 611/293

[70] CR 737/93
[71] CR 1570/71
[72] Z 789(sm)
[73] CR 1520/from Box 62
[74] Reference to the red Twinlock binders may reveal more detailed evidence of women's involvement.
[75] CR 367/116/4
[76] CR 815/117-119 and /120 - 127
[77] CR 2546
[78] PH 352/187/284
[79] PH 350/2227 - 8
[80] PH 406/157
[81] PH 680
[82] CR 2151/138
[83] CR 556/66 Box 93

Research by Alternative Strategies

There will be some Warwickshire women for whom there are very few direct references in the indexes of the WCRO. Unfortunately, it is in the nature of an archival collection, bearing in mind the haphazard character of document survival and deposition, for even quite famous people to be poorly represented. Their papers might not have survived, or might be held elsewhere. Their names might be mentioned in the records of the societies or committees to which they belonged; letters from them might turn up tantalisingly in other people's collections, but there might not be enough material in the WCRO to warrant detailed study. Students hoping to find large collections in connection with Lady Lucy of Charlecote (1803-1889) or Frances, Countess of Warwick (1861-1938), will be disappointed.

A user may wish to research a particular woman for whom there appears to be no obvious archival material in the WCRO. The method outlined below will be helpful in obtaining information through various channels. For example, Christobel Wheatley of Berkswell Hall was typical of a woman of her era who was well known in the county and local social circles, but was a parochial rather than a national figure. In common with many of her upper-class contemporaries, she went to Italy during the early days of World War One and worked for the Red Cross. During her time there she met the Wheatley sisters and later met and married their brother, Colonel Wheatley. She led the typical social life of the leisured class: hunting, giving parties and going to balls, entertaining and buying designer clothes. She joined the Woodmen of Arden, an archery club, where she won a garnet bracelet. Her husband was a Conservative County Councillor, and after his death she took over and for many years was a strong representative. After her first year in office, the Labour candidate, a railway signalman who contested the seat, congratulated her because he believed she had done well.

Christobel Wheatley was not a believer in party politics, which she felt devalued political philosophy. She reflected the assumptions of the time when the Lady of the Manor was looked up to and respected because of who she was and not what she was. She accepted the obligations of her position as a matter of course. She was imperious, strong-minded and charming, and the people of Berkswell believed they were fortunate in having Mrs Wheatley to defend and protect them. She always considered local people, and involved herself in all the local clubs and committees. Mrs Wheatley was Chairman of the Records and Museums Committee in the 1960s. She was Chairman of the Berkswell Girls' Club and also of the Parochial Church Council, which always met at Berkswell Hall. There was no central heating in the Hall and Mrs Wheatley would pile on layers of clothes for warmth, and expect the other members to do likewise and not to complain. She was a great traveller, and on her return she would give a talk, illustrated with slides. She was a much respected figure and was sadly missed when she moved to a retirement home in Dorset.

Assuming that the user has a specific woman in mind and knows a reasonable amount already, finding-aids and sources used to compile similar information are listed below:

1. Visit WCRO and look in Names Index.

2. Consult General Index (if a landed family).

3. Follow up subject's interests in the Subject Index for example,

political involvement or voluntary work. In the case of Mrs Wheatley, it is known that she was involved in the Berkswell Girls' Club, and records relating to this are deposited at the WCRO.[1] Lateral thinking might suggest that a woman of her background would be a staunch member and supporter of the local church, so an examination of the Berkswell Parochial Church Council Minutes could be rewarding.

4. Local newspapers are worth looking through for reports of her activities.

5. Other records of particular relevance. If it is already known that the subject had been a County Councillor, County Council records should be consulted.

6. In some cases, the Wills Index might be useful.

Users should not have a preconceived idea of where their research should lead; they should be prepared to follow their own instincts and respond to the findings as they are discovered.

Reference
[1] CR 1602

"Darling Daisy", the Countess of Warwick
(1861-1938)

Quixotic, extravagant, the mistress of the Prince of Wales and a dramatic convert to socialism in 1895, the Countess nevertheless had some solid achievements to her name. In the field of opportunities for women she supported colleges for the training of women in agriculture and horticulture, first at Reading and then at Studley in Warwickshire.

Lady Warwick and son.

Conclusion

We have consistently underlined that this *Guide* contains a selection only of the rich variety of material available in the Warwickshire County Record Office. Students should remember that there are many sources of information relating to the history of women that are not yet in the Record Office. Oral history is another valuable source, and it can be rewarding to talk to local people. Also, local history groups and historians can be helpful. Artefacts and ephemera relating to the subject of the research are sometimes to be found in museums.

We hope that this publication will encourage people to explore the fascinating and largely ignored subject of women's history, and thereby to increase their knowledge and understanding of our heritage.

Great care has been taken in compiling the historical information contained in this book which is believed to be correct. No responsibility can be accepted for any error.